Next to Nothing

CHRIS AGEE was born in 1956 and grew up in Massachusetts, Rhode Island and New York. He attended Harvard University and since 1979 has lived in Ireland. He is the author of two collections of poems, *In the New Hampshire Woods* (The Dedalus Press, 1992) and *First Light* (The Dedalus Press, 2003), as well as the editor of *Scar on the Stone: Contemporary Poetry from Bosnia* (Bloodaxe Books, 1998, Poetry Society Recommended Translation), *Unfinished Ireland: Essays on Hubert Butler* (Irish Pages, 2003) and *The New North: Contemporary Poetry from Northern Ireland* (Wake Forest University Press, 2008). He reviews regularly for *The Irish Times* and is the Editor of *Irish Pages*, a journal of contemporary writing based at the Linen Hall Library, Belfast.

Also by Chris Agee

POETRY
    In the New Hampshire Woods (The Dedalus Press, 1992)
    First Light (The Dedalus Press, 2003)

AS EDITOR
    Scar on the Stone: Contemporary Poetry from Bosnia (Bloodaxe
        Books, 1998)
    Unfinished Ireland: Essays on Hubert Butler (Irish Pages, 2003)
    The New North: Contemporary Poetry from Northern Ireland (Wake
        Forest University Press, 2008)

Next to Nothing

CHRIS AGEE

CAMBRIDGE

PUBLISHED BY SALT PUBLISHING
PO Box 937, Great Wilbraham, Cambridge CB21 5JX United Kingdom

© Chris Agee, 2008

The right of Chris Agee to be identified as the
author of this work has been asserted by him in accordance
with Section 77 of the Copyright, Designs and Patents Act 1988.

Salt Publishing 2008

Printed in Great Britain by the MPG Books Group, Bodmin and King's Lynn.

Typeset in Swift 9.5 / 13

ISBN 978 1 84471 489 6 hardback

Salt Publishing Ltd gratefully acknowledges
the financial assistance of Arts Council England

1 3 5 7 9 8 6 4 2

In memory of Miriam Aoife Agee

12 i 1997 – 4 iv 2001

Contents

Notes and Acknowledgements

Some of these poems first appeared in *Fortnight*, *The Harvard Review*, *Honest Ulsterman*, *The Irish Times*, *Limestone*, *Poetry Ireland Review*, *Studies*, *Tabla*, *Tiferet*, *The Yellow Nib* and *Times Literary Supplement*.

"In Prvo Selo", "In the Adriatic" and "Attic Grace" appeared in the anthology *Wingspan: A Dedalus Sampler*, edited by Pat Boran (The Dedalus Press, 2006). "Sebald" and "Alpine Interlude" were included in the anthology *Magnetic North: The Emerging Poets*, edited by John Brown (Lagan Press, 2006). "Alpine Interlude" also appeared in *Something Beginning with P*, edited by Seamus Cashman (O'Brien Press, 2004).

Seven sections of "In the Adriatic" were used by the Irish composer Elaine Agnew in a composition of the same name commissioned by RTÉ. It was first performed by the contemporary music ensemble, Concorde, in July 2006.

"Stellata" is a variety of magnolia. "Qi" is a word of Chinese origin for the life-force. In California, an "estero" is a sea-inlet of wetlands; in Ireland, "machair" is the sandy pasturage found behind dunes. "Ragusa" is the Italian name for Dubrovnik. The dates given in "Heartscapes" refer to the moment of genesis and not necessarily of composition.

At Bethlehem Nursery

The frost this morning was thick, Byzantine,
Coating an infinite wicker of grass leaves, blades of daffodil,
Old November leaves curled like lips of conch,
Side view mirror fingered clear in the early morning

Eternally new. Quintessential Irish chill, unvanquished bluish-white
Under sleepers of shadow on sun-warmed verges,
The visitation, the annunciation of night—fog's delicate lacework
Breathed out by the Gulf Steam's circumpolar Ariel.

MID-MARCH 2001

A Bouquet from Miriam

I

Violet and primroses brought through the night from Donegal
To be laid near her coffin-plate splashed with a quicksilver sprinkle.

II

After a week's Shiva, we pick wood-anemone for our box of ashes
And let go her fluttering soul. *I see the Styx at Minnowburn Beeches.*

III

A month on, parachutes from the dead moons of dandelions
Glistening like thistledown on the lost air of her departed time.

MAY 2001

Heaney at Struga

When Heaney rose at Struga, two days after
Receiving the Golden Wreath in the great hall

Of the House of Poetry, and spoke
Before a front row full of politicians

In a Macedonia on the cusp of war, aisles aswarm
With moths fluttering in floodlight, sweet night breezes

Off the waters of Lake Ochrid, of how
Persuaded by the power of his art

Hades had stilled his kingdom of shades
For Orpheus descending to the underworld:

Axion's wheel halted, Sisyphus suspended,
The stopped spindles of the spinning Fates:

His unparalleled lyre held like a buckler
Leading her soul up the dark slope towards the light

Of new life, the human love and the human fear
Whose backward glance cost him his beloved

Eurydice forever: I thought, then, of the weight
Slipping, piggybacking my own daughter

Out of the ultimate pit, dark crypt of her bedroom,
To five more minutes, even, of life's warm brow . . .

AUGUST 2001

[3]

Depths

In Mayo,
on one of those

beaches where blanket
bog runs down

to the strand, beetling
the hard sand's stumps

of bog-pine garlanded
with bladderwrack,

a businessman unearthed,
on the tideline,

two Celtic torcs,
their gold

lambency emerging,
so I imagined,

from the black
Ireland

of time passed, which
made me think, too,

of the shining hoards
of imagery, or love's presence

lifted clear of the calendar
depths of untarnished memory.

The awful Saturday
was the last day

of March, the ides
of her little life.

Chaucer's April,
sweetest month,

I walked out of that last room
to hailstones

on the windshield,
a branch down

in the spangled
garden of the world

left four days before,
to the new place

I would never leave.
In May

I waited for a sign,
small nymph

out of the bog-pool
of death: the mayfly's

grannon or iron blue.
Ascendant

June and July, lush
Mediterranean twins,

when everything,
it seemed, led back

to her:
a doe in the Catskills

on a lawn's far shore;
the Žrnovo garden's

small, delicate
bejewelled insects

and butterflies
never failing

to remind me
of Miriam's brief

but exquisite life
(as if, indeed, this

was the real insight—
in its shadow—

into life after death).
Struga, mid-August,

I watched from a balcony
a phalanx of belligerent crows

smudge the morning dusk
over Ochrid's glistening

mother-of-pearl sheen.
When the Eleventh

struck out of the blue
yonder, a bright

bolt of dust, I learnt
the limits of empathy:

to be there, truly,
was to *be* there. Fall

was Old
New England

clement, an Irish
Indian summer,

October leaf
yellowing slowly,

too slowly, to
the bare branches

of despair,
November's last

winter primrose—
planted her sick-day—

ragged, now, as the heart.
An empty playground

in December,
wan London

illuminations
on the face of a wall,

the same sky
over Auschwitz;

in the mind's eye
seeing her small soul

before the Babylon
of the Tate Modern,

the Dynamo's
excathedral ziggurat,

rivets like dies,
birch and the brown

river rhombus lit
into swirling latte,

imagined mudlarks
still haunting trove

on its twilit slob.
Now upcoming January's

the Ground Zero
of no epiphany,

slouching towards un-
imaginable March,

death like a voice
in the Otis lift

sounding to no one,
or a belfry bisected

by the empty sky,
the bitterness

which will never wash
out of the shining blue.

DECEMBER 2001

Sebald

1944–2001

On and off, I had been musing about vistas
Of simultaneity: the continuum between, say,

In a natural sense, fresh graves in Afghanistan
And the abysmal plain on the Marianas Trench

Lit by the spectral traceries of bioluminescence; or,
In the social, sipping coffee as Srebrenica happened

In waves of twenty-plus. How—at any one time—everything
Is happening in a single world-image like tens of millions

Of words in a Babel of thousands of tongues coexisting
In its archive of consciousness. That interior Friday

In the Year of the Buddhas, it might have happened
As I paused for a moment at a window over Royal Avenue

Or collected my daughter's last photographs amid the sad
Crepuscule of the framing shop. Now, over coffee, reading

Of *seiceamóir* and *cuileann* in *Trees of Ireland*,
I think of his radiant endings: *a last glimpse of the land*

now being lost forever and *reaching the town*
as evening began to fall: and hope

His noble German span and hers in miniature
Are travelling forever into the dark land of eternal light.

DECEMBER 2001

[10]

Next to Nothing

According to the Sufis, *suffering is a special sign*
Of divine favour: so a new friend's letter

Tells me, verifying (almost) its theme of a new life
In the spirit of death. Once again, I hardly know

What to make of such an extraordinary gloss:
Which reminds me, like all the rest, of the human

Barnacled to the great right whale of Heidegger's Being,
Touching it has no idea what osmosis: or rounded,

Uncovered stones like Jesus's writing on the sand
At the vast strand at Magheraroarty. Everyone arrives

Into the cloud of my real unknowing, hoping
To make good the camp ruination

Of the small Taj Mahal of Miriam's life,
The Mogul invader of memory's love; even so, truth

To tell, there is strange comfort in the sage
Belief of others, like Rusmir's in Sarajevo,

A stone's throw from the market stalls ghosted
With the Second Law of Thermodynamics: suspected Sufi

Who has never written. Knowing myself nothing;
Nothing sure; or next-to-nothing. That is all.

JANUARY 2002

Attic Grace

The moon is more beautiful than any nation state . . .
                                          Is this, then,
The litmus of civilization? Islam's beloved crescent more beautiful even

Than Mohammed? As being must be to belief, to revelation?
The new moon to the reckonings of Mecca? Alabaster discus

As pitted as an Attic face . . .
O pristine planet of dust and vellum
                                        O inhuman gem

The Tulip Tree

Is what the woman said she called it, the countrywoman
With sad perse eyes and a mane of greying ringlets

Who sold us a small magnolia and told us of her daughter's
Slow death of MS. I thought of the gathering dark

In the dusk of a sugar-plum evening with Miriam
When the treetops, we said, were dusted in icing

She longed to touch: huge snowflakes drifting
Through black panels of our café bay, a celeste's hour

Magicking childhood's storm-bound sofa. What would she make
(Have made) of the waxen blush of the tulip tree? Today

The memorial stellata of another, like a great bloom of time—
Petals fallen into moments, sudden freshet of sunlight,

The mahogany spreads of Shamrock Compost—was planted
A year to the noon of her death's end to all moods and tenses.

MAY 2002

Life

In broad midmorning, a wild streak of handsome ginger,
Reynard of the suburban bins, in a lull in the traffic,

Ventured the gap ahead and leapt a high stone wall
To the den-paradise of Riddel Woods. Why's the natural

So consoling? It should surely be otherwise: what can
One life mean in Hubble's cosmological hall-of-mirrors,

Dark matter and curved space, light bent into
Replications of galaxies, the entropy of the Big Bang?

And *When time and space began*, what can *that* mean?
Yet this hour on Ireland there's still the azure-green

Pearl of the world: life's microcosm, the conscious imago
Like a jellyfish drifting (and maybe parallax millions of them)

Through the blackened depths, hot-air balloon of the lit gift
A helium teardrop in the universal darkness of "God"?

The Apocalypse of Fishes

Beautiful fish, sunlight streaming
Into vivid iridescence. First gate,
First stall: turbot and halibut, a huge conger,

Blueblack mackerel and silvery herring,
The abstract oysters. Glassy sea-bass eyes
And red mullet mounted on beds of ice;

Slow-motion dumbshow of lobsters
Entangled in seaweed; crabs packed
In bladderwrack, their Portavogie crates

Like cattletrucks. Zero metaphysics,
I feel its brute truth—the one life, ended
Or ebbing: a death scene, blood-spattered

And ice-bound, like the moment itself.

The August Dream

Suddenly you were back—coming towards me, running,
Nóirín in your wake at a distance, signalling the joy

To an unseen someone on the right—Sally perhaps—
The dream capturing all of you exactly : chunky white trainers,

The checked winter coat—open—slipping off your shoulders,
The flying blond strands, the gay and husky laugh

And face of love as you leapt straight into my arms
To announce you had only got out the bathroom window

And "the commoner"—by which I understood, rightly somehow,
"the janitor"—had . . . but there it ended, too strong, it seemed,

To remain untested in sleep and so jerked back to the blue
Adriatic pane at seven a.m. Yet through another hour's

Willed oblivion of slumber, it was inexpressibly wonderful
To have you even so, an ambrosia that might keep me going

Another year, nectar like the hummingbird hawk-moth sucks
At sundown from the yellows and scarlets of an unnamed flower

Still in sunshine, a return to a land of happiness out of the hardened
Soreness sitting always like a shadow's gargoyle on my solar plexus . . .

As on the afternoon before, when scything a year's hay
In the dwarf orchard of almonds and walnuts, I happened on

A praying mantis, immaculate jade green, sunning on a wall rock
Spotted by umber lichen, and remembered its role as last summer's

Image of reincarnation to another state, and thought and felt,
Sitting on the wall, how wonderful it was to have you there

Even so—after nature—transmogrified by a moment's wing-flick
To the old world's bower where your living life was with us still.

AUGUST 2002

Mirage

The road on Mljet . . . it might almost make me a believer. I mean
The dirt road rising, dipping and twisting along the Small Lake

Glistening with shallows of chalk, jade and greengage
Glimpsed through the undergrowth and Aleppo pines

Whose shadows ink its rough camber. For two summers
It's happened towards four, or thereabouts: shimmering time

When the last stragglers, honeyed with memory,
A day's small wonders, wend their way dreamily

To the waiting ferry. There's a whiff, perhaps, of brine
Off the breezy tidal channel, and the woods still sing

With hoarse rattles in an endless racket of cricket-chirr.
And near the portable WC where the stairs rise steeply

To the right, into the cool fragrance of the pines,
A memory of both of you, hand-in-hand, heading

Towards the first step, shimmers into feeling so strongly
It's as if I'm seeing a moment's mirage with a second sight . . .

Then back to nothing, the beautiful world
Whose condition is doubt, like a physicist of memorials

Leaving a crop circle dewdropped in the field of the present:
The absence of God is God enough

The Science of Lampshades

I had just been reading of Newton's three laws of motion
In a science column of *The Irish Times*—my metaphysic of

Morning coffee, like an inmate's cigarette—and was shaving
In the usual place, the mirror propped in the window—

A cup of toothbrushes, soap dish, shaving cream, tubes and mug
Bound to the sink in the Moon-Earth ratio of gravitation—

And was deep into a riff on the black box of life, our cell of light,
Thinking of how imagination was simply the space outside

(How the very idea of *answers* was absurd and anthropocentric),
How its purpose was simply to interrogate the Why, or even

Whether there was a Why, how the Why was a province
On which the How of science, its hubris, had no purchase—

Right as all this was happening in the bright mercurial
Ghosts between the synapses, fibre-optics of the spirit,

The ovoid bathroom lampshade, a large paper globe, dropped
For the first time since unfolded and hung up round the light

A decade or more before. I thought in a flash, unwilling,
If it was ever to happen, this was Miriam telling me

She was near, tapping through the prison of natural fact
Her only route from the dead: one of my Testaments

To the restructurings of tragedy in the sorrow of aftermath—
The rest being godspeak, mantlings of human projection,

The Panglossian claptrap of fruit flies at the windows of Auschwitz . . .
And so the whole thing seemed natural but the surprise billowed

As I paused, dusted swiftly, lifted it and saw in this cold cell
    sheltering
Beauty and joy—in its silent replacement—a metaphor for the space
    outside.

November 2002

Heartscapes
for Nóirín

There is a light that reaches us only after a long time.
Dust, dust, and a few lines mortal and evanescent.
— DONALD JUSTICE

Like an *alef*

the bright morning
contrail
seen
over months
from shadowy rooms

7 JANUARY 2003

The sandpile

in Croatia
day after day
of pure life
next to their
Museum
of toy relics

I wish

to live
near
the coffin
of small details

Written in sleep
12 JANUARY 2003
(Miriam's birthday)

[25]

As ever

fresh and new-minted
the face
I love
in the gloom
of every dawn-dusk

14 JANUARY 2003

The word

Death
so old
there is no
first
etymology

14 JANUARY 2003

According

to Amichai
God is
change
and Death
is His
prophet

14 January 2003

The yellow

gantries
now conceptual
the last ship
from the shipyard
it all
becomes
a period

21 JANUARY 2003

Pain

like love's
Doppler Effect
a sudden onrush
of a passing
memory

21 JANUARY 2003

O the evening

of the striped snails
on the move at dusk
in dunes
cooled and dewy
then the strand's
dead seal
lit preternatural
by the sea's
golden foil

21 JANUARY 2003

Still stunned

I gaze
through the glass
of the barber's
balancing
on the edge
between the wound's
wellspring
and the stilled surface
of living

St Brigid's Day 2003

One

of the old beauties
of the world
a breath
of fresh snow
on a clear day
the ferry's horn
on Korčula
like a young window
thrown open

4 FEBRUARY 2003

Your face

swims
in the window
where I wave
at the childminder's
new child

Your shoes

still there
left
duck-toed
on the second stair
I bow
ceremonious
and Japanese
to kiss
the space
and time
of your presence

9 FEBRUARY 2003

Baby clothes

in the hall
a sailor suit
the beach day's
bonnet
bibs and socks
her little shoes
which once trod
the world
deflated
without her
spirit

14 FEBRUARY 2003

Your life

left
sombre and deserted
like the Coroner's
Court
one flawless dusk
a winter beauty
outwith Belfast
Full Moon
and the pinprick
of Venus

15 FEBRUARY 2003

A whole

lifetime
without Dotie
like the rainbow's
adieu
over the Village
bridge
the afternoon
of your death

16 FEBRUARY 2003

The worst

of the worst
was when
I lifted each lid
and saw
the blue eyes
I loved
more than life
stilled
forever
on the splattered bed

3 MARCH 2003

Incommunicable

Shock and awe

or better
pity and sorrow
for the boy
with the back of his head
blown off

31 MARCH 2003

[41]

The Day

of memory
and death
that old dew of youth
on grass
the petals
of magnolia
already falling

4 APRIL 2003
(Miriam's deathday)

Birdsong

at dawn
like a far-off
heavenly
music
of the dead

4 APRIL 2003
(Miriam's deathday)

Hard and bare

light
of North America
on an apron
of the New World
of death
and the final
mystery

Logan Airport, Boston
8 APRIL 2003

In the end

you still
live
in me
like clouds
in a vernal pond
whose sky
has vanished

Massachusetts
13 APRIL 2003

[45]

Old lizard

heavy-lidded
and somnolent
in the sun
not confirming
not denying
the divine origin
of being

Massachusetts
14 APRIL 2003

The once

seamless
blue
now rent
with the contrail
of sorrow's shining
cicatrix

Massachusetts
15 APRIL 2003

I imagine

her
as she might have been
golden girl
the two older magnolias
siding the portico
at Andover
where I watched
Euripides
on the grass
one sweet May

Phillips Academy, Massachusetts
25 APRIL 2003

It arced slowly

up and up
a baseball's
parabola
into the twilit
Upper Deck
where
(never closer)
Dad
fielded it
for me

Yankee Stadium
3 MAY 2003

[49]

Its life

is ending
blossom of
horsechestnut
that dripped
on my cheek
from a bough
high above

Beautiful little violets

heart-shaped leaves
shamrocks
of deepest mauve
whose time
is brief
but even so
perennial

Washington, DC
7 MAY 2003

Sick

sick
sick
each dawn
as if
I bide
my time
unto Death

Washington, DC
7 MAY 2003

Texts texts

next
to nothing
a Book of Hours
from Troyes
first edition
of *Leaves of Grass*
a worm-eaten
Nuremberg Chronicle
with blank pages
for the coming centuries
before
the known
apocalypse
of Death's Dance
and black lozenges
for the open graves

University of Iowa Library
12 MAY 2003

Why

did I imagine you
at this old Quaker school
in Iowa
still gracing
the world
you never had
like light
trembling inside
on the meeting-house's
jambs and sills and sashes

West Branch, Iowa
12 MAY 2003

Nightmare

Liberia
where "the god"
of Abraham
turns away
again
(and again)
from "creation"

Berkeley
15 MAY 2003

My father's ghost

in naval khaki
astride a knoll
in Presidio
City Lights and Ferlinghetti
tablecloths
of checkered linen
the good life
of other days
now dusty traces
of the eternal
annihilation

San Francisco
20 MAY 2003

Like Darwin

I turn
from the church door
"Restez-y"
says Prévert
of the divine
though I remember
too
the First Letter
of John
where the hope is
all love
is one

Boston
24 MAY 2003

How clear

it seems
the last Thursday
before your death
you and "Jakey"
on bikes
me behind walking
watching
your every twist and turn
along paths
under Ormeau's great-blossoming chestnuts
aware
consciously
of some new plateau
of contentment
cut short
for good
by the One
apocalypse

Boston
25 MAY 2003

Off season

my spirit
the light
on the weather-beaten
grey float
lifted for winter
the Lake a balm
the woods lush
the mountains inky
and May's puff-flecked skies
it has all
happened
in six years
experience
is
solitude
of driftwood

Squam Lake, New Hampshire
30 MAY 2003

The empty bench

rotted
on the dock
where my father sat
where you sat
the same light
trembling
in the corner
before your
coffin came

Squam Lake, New Hampshire
30 MAY 2003

I stare

at wisps
of cumulus
above
a baleen
of palm fronds
back to a bench
in Korčula
you were with us
that summer too
a small *sprog*
hidden to
the company
now the world's
stripped-out
luminously calm
bare
but beautiful
without
you

Korčula, Croatia
14 AUGUST 2003

I heard

tell
of Mrs Kelly
seen
often
in Derry City's
cemetery
on a cold night
with blankets
to keep
her son
warm
and know now
I have not
remembered
enough

Dublin
3 OCTOBER 2003
(Michael Kelly, aged 17, murdered 30 January 1972)

The Dark

Zone
is where
we spend
our lives
like deep sea
luminescence
dreaming a dawn
of elvers
in a shimmering
Sargasso
of the dead
Above

Dromore, Co Down
23 OCTOBER 2003
(Seamus Mackin's funeral)

[63]

Winter sun

low
and blinding
over the place
of your funeral
at the end
I'll be glad
to go
into
its helium
glow

1 December 2003

The window

where you died
under
the Belfast hills
olive-gnarled
and snow-capped
the hospital's
orbital art
pure blue
launchpad
into nothingness
of being

28 FEBRUARY 2004

The morning moon

in blue
Omega
of the day
like the dead
here
and not here
real
and unreal
banished by
the daily
afternoon
pure and bright
ready for exit
at the moment's
gate
the last poem
always unwritten

Ormeau Park
11 DECEMBER 2003

Winter moon

Islam's silver
sliver
depleted
to its bright
scoop's
nothingness
of memory

DECEMBER 2004

Eight years

ago
this day
beautiful Miriam
entered
our light

12 JANUARY 2005

A dream

somewhere hot
and blue
with mountains
the Caribbean
maybe
Peggy
and the Guirovs
around about
Miriam goes out
before we're up
never
to return

16 JANUARY 2005

The wounded day

Saturday
afternoon
naps
threadbare
heartache
still unburied

22 JANUARY 2005

Your cousin

blond
and wispy
the same pale
delicacy
at the christening
of another life
oil of catechumens
chrism
of salvation
reminding me
more and more
of you
more and more
of not-you
inside

At Clodiagh's christening
13 FEBRUARY 2005

Notes

from the hospital
on the top shelf
at the office
by a diary
open still
at a week in April
to Croatia
the Easter trip
forever ahead

3 MARCH 2005

Reading

the Obituaries
I look always
for
the great
achievement
of children

5 MARCH 2005

It

never
gets done
it sits
on the desk
covered in dust
the notebook
of "Memories"
I'm unable
to face

12 MARCH 2005

Mist

at Easter
a magnolia
below
the three processions
round Žrnovo
chapel
beautiful hosannas
and alleluias
but I hold out
on the back row
though afterwards
violets and dog daisies
and others unnamed
fringe the ancient
road of creation

Žrnovo, Croatia
27 MARCH 2005

The embers

downstairs
still redden in the dark
heart
of memory's
night

Žrnovo, Croatia
6 APRIL 2005

I missed

your stellata
this year
only a baker's
dozen were left
one still
with the ghost
of a fragrance

6 April 2005

Here

not here
is
the one
truth

Dublin
27 MAY 2005

[78]

History's

No Entry
dreams
like the death
they replicate

Written in sleep
9 APRIL 2006
(Miriam's funeral-day)

I come

under the sun
birdsong and birches
the white foam
of life
last daffodils
and the dew
again
delicate
on grasses and petals
like perspiration
on your sickbed brow

FINIS

Heartlands

1 Observatory, Empire State Building

Night shimmerings. Sahara of million-fold
mirage. Or cooling lava in full flow,
its salamander glows. Down below, shadowy
geometries, a bird fluttering above the stone

evolution of humanity, dazzling capital
of capitalism. Surely it will outlast us,
the miracle of its dinosaur-flight
against our chthonic powers, all idiolect

of microcosm. As, say, Grand Central
at flowering Park, where blossoms drift
in time and space, its verdigris
dome like a Greek mirror

inscribed with mythologies; or Uptown
at Yankee Stadium, the rusting El
and rotted, ramshackle cistern, Hopperesque,
still shadowing the platform, sad and tired

now, like the heart, where Mantle
was once eternal
as boyhood; or Downtown, tonight, whose rising
half-light fogs of street light, windows

banked as ocean liners', the obsidian
polish of the Two Rivers, bespeak, surely, the true
apocalyptic note that sea-girts the tongue's
universal grammar for the human moment.

Vietnam's wound. Polished black
Bangalore granite, its oblique angles
a hanger's incision, tapering obsidian
blades of a Shaker rocker—the globe's biggest

tombstone. No symbols, no statements: just
the silence of death, word without
etymology or gloss, word most truly
itself. Via the nearby Book of the Dead

I locate the place (arranged in the order
"they were taken from us") of the name
Robert Ransom, whose death's single
rippling heartbreak brushed my boyhood

in May of '68. Forever, his
will stare towards the land
of the living, meeting our clouded eyes.
Then the Lincoln Memorial,

its ghosts from death-soaked Gettysburg,
the kitsch of Korea's, a World War Two
work-in-progress, sad forgotten rhododendrons
round the domed doughboy monument,

plus legions more
on the rolling greens of Arlington,
a continent of griefs—vanished
and living—beyond the Potomac's

Indian syllables: nothing less
than Washington's federal necropolis
consecrating the collective
landscape of its blood-hemmed nation-state.

3 Amish Quilt, Kalona

Bruegel in Iowa . . . I am told the Amish don
their best blues and whites and blacks, to skate
on the small ponds of vanished prairielands
checkerboarded with fields themselves etched

with fallow swathes of watercourses. Is their faith,
stylized, the mystery of self-limitation, America turned
inside out, something sealed against the World's *imperium*
they've unburdened, I inhabit—like those New

World monasteries, the Shaker villages? After a walk
in encroaching prairie woods, spring leaves revealing
themselves, a sprinkle of violets, Canada geese,
cornfields of shorn stubble, off a dirt road

in a landscape of silver silos and weather-beaten,
windswept white barns, storm-darkened skies,
the Nineteenth Century looked out of a bonneted face
pausing over the handle-bar of a manual lawnmower:

Old Europe's folk sense of time-in-place, the same
I felt at *Yoder's Antiques*, when antique Kalona quilts
were unfolded, with names like "Sunshine & Shadow"
and "Cactus Bowl". I bought one with two names and later

when I unfurled its denims and ochres (Jasper Johns *avant*
la lettre) on the stairwell of the International Writers Program,
(seeing an icon for my prairie time), to be hung somewhere central,
"Stair-Steps", as I opted, got the staff's spontaneous applause.

4 Limantour Beach, Point Reyes

We reached its Pacific breakers. At last I
dove into the globe's icy eyeball. Behind us
the Marin Hills were California heaven,
Qi of eucalyptus and blue: turkey vultures,

poppies and lupine, Steller's jay, oaks, redwood, bay,
Mexican pine, quail, a red-tailed hawk. Out of Rwanda
Jean-Marie, trousers rolled up, touched the sea-foam
for the first time. On its blank sands, the fresh world's

tabula rasa, a Rosetta Stone for silence, transponder-
and-float stood in for Man Friday's footprint halting
my single track of marks. Three brown pelicans
skimmed the given of the spindrift. Dunes and estero,

the scrubland and the Hills, in ocean's foundations
land's *imperium* ended: a mesa of dreams. Even I could glimpse
in cognate breakers, some vision of Miłosz or Jeffers unlanguaged
—unwilled, undone—by the cold sea-wash at continent's end.

5 Boston Common

A Shaw Memorial for the Iraqi dead? *One overhears the art*
of the single voice. In Baghdad a gold Akkadian harp
is looted and vanishes; in a refrigerated truck, a small boy
stiffens on a pile of corpses. *It was the protest of the individual soul*

which is never wasted. Not a stone's throw from where
divines hung an Irish "witch"—their first—Miriam leapfrogged
below the kidney-shaped Frog Pond the last summer before
her death. *Whether one makes things happen, one can, at least,*

say what happened, what was: and that is something
towards the what-becomes-what-is. So let us call it that—
a spade a spade—let us make it personal, *let us now praise*
infamous men, their famous victory, saying what was was this:

A servant's war. Rumsfeld's war. A servile war.

MAY–JUNE 2003

Alpine Interlude

When we reached the mountain bog in the saddle
Of Jackson, and saw the heads of thousands
Of cotton sedge trembling and bobbing, letting go

Their fleecy tufts like thistledown in Ireland
Over archipelagos of blackbrown peat sediment—
I thought, after a while, of those days in Kosovo: life

Essential in its passing, its beauty, its tragedy. But first
Pausing long trail minutes, the boy becalmed on
Planks of the bog bridge, seeing mountain cranberry,

Pale laurel, Canada mayflower, windy Appalachian bog
Rimmed by Labrador tea, the sweetness of the moment
Reminded me of Miriam's life, its brevity and softness,

Its summery interlude, its sunniness stretching
Out to the unending dark dwarf balsam fir-trees
And the great universe bowl of the White Mountains

In sheer airy blue outline, the cumuli sailing in
Puffs of snapdragon and Hiroshima . . . with which,
Nonetheless, in the mind's eye, her time seemed one.

JULY 2003

[87]

Sea-campion

So back
we come, again,

to the eternal
homeland, this time

the morning machair
right at the end

of summer. Harebell,
hawksbit, dead

thistle and its thistledown,
lady's bedstraw,

bird's-foot trefoil,
wild mint, clumps

of *the hungry grass*—
light's windy atmospherics

in the ecosystem
of spirit, a dry

Irish tundra plain
that deepens

with each time's
time—all laid out

as if on linens
for an hour's shroud.

～

Days
of heaven, pure

deal strand,
a grain of hues,

sand, iron,
loosened beige.

A round stone
sits in its shadow's

parabola; a lifesaver
in dunes

hitched to two boards,
rope coiled

in a diamond frame,
like a Celtic cross

silhouettes
cumuli and blue;

a sea-rod's
encrusted sceptre.

Every beach
is the end,

he says,
of land and sea,

where some say
we began.

~

The bright red buoy
has vanished. The other,

rusted orb, has rolled
to a grassy rest

at the foot of the slope.
My stone throne's overgrown.

Only the telephone pole's
limp basketball net

seems left from
a stage-set of moments

where the kids played
round the hostel's

arcade. *Pity what little
made them happy.*

~

An old pain now.
Revisiting

sites of joy,
where a seal's eyes

once twinkled.
Transliterate to

the present
moment: reeds in wind,

a brock flees to its sett
out of bogbean

and flags. The huge
rock-pool at Rosguill,

a sunken
seaweed garden,

blooms of
kelps and bladderwrack,

sea-lettuce and dulse
stranded in the sun, stilled

as memories in
a deep pool

of griefs,
sandy bottom

cast in its patina
of old bronze. But behind,

the cleft rocks are still
thickly shaggy with

untouched lichens,
chalk-green, orangey-gold,

sparking the thought
of poetry's sustenance

in the hard matter
of the world. And one

gorgeous flower, still
unnamed, I have never

seen. Time
enough, still,

before saying it all
goodbye.

September 2003

The Zebra Finches

Whether it was an Arctic cold-snap, or
A day's empty tray, or simply allotted
Old age, or maybe all three, clearly

The bird was ill, huddled with Milky,
Loyal mate, at the bottom of the cage
In their little world, its light and presence,

Its daily being. So I hastened to fetch
Millet-seeds and a doll's cup of water
As if she'd picnic on a paper towel, trying

To feed the creature in the cup of my palm;
Seeing, soon enough, I was expending its final
Energies now mustering to the upright, ebbing

In the mortal coil, stock-still in the last dignity
Of flickering life.
                    In any event, inattentive
As ever, I went down to the TV and watched

Tales of the Holocaust, one in particular
Amazing even the Teller six decades hence—
The children locked in a credenza, Mother's murder,

Dead silence, the crying of Father: a train
To Treblinka, rotted floorboards, a drop
Onto the rushing sleepers and thence

To the woods: wanderings in Warsaw,
Pants shat, white sheets: did it all come
To this a lifetime ago?
                        When I returned

She was dead, a keeled-over featherweight
In deathly solitude, her picnic bird's-feet
Clutching the nothingness of air. Milky silent

On a trapeze above, death-night of my Father
Two years on. Birds too, I saw—as if fixing
A *memento mori*—have swift rigor mortis.

Soulmates

You're nothing now. I'm close, though, close
As the five-o'clock shadow on a photocopy's
Gnomon of nothingness. I gave you life, dear ghost,

Then Death came from a detour's first glimpse
Amidst sunshadowy haymakers in Montenegro.
I passed on unscathed . . .
                              In your room's aftermath,

Love's amber, still lifes at a standstill, chill as a crypt,
Cold heaven of atoms stardusting space, or a moth's
Herculaneum on 9/XI: a Shaker box of ashes,

Dried wood anemone from the first week, party dress,
Dolls and toys, *Babar* book, a puppet. Still, enough to fill
A lifetime. I'm a lake of swans mirroring the vanished

Weathers of your time. Dark elephant tears, a world without
Birds or frost, the cut scent of winter grass. I see us slipping
Down into nothing under a pewter sheen on Belfast Lough.

FEBRUARY 2004

Tea-herb

Pressed flower, this sprig's a souvenir of days fresh with grief
Whose final cruelty was the bitter herb of desiccation, when death
Once came strange as afternoon gusts from a dusky cloudburst

Whose zephyrs (while I was out) lifted from a table—overshooting
My room's balcony—three pages of a friend's speech. One landed
By an underground entrance, another on a grassy knoll near

An empty perimeter, but the last had vanished—to dusk was lost
As Eurydice, not found on patrolled grounds: a launch teetering
On the cusp of civil war, her paper ghost blown off by windiness.

(Struga Poetry Festival)
MARCH 2004

Crolly Woods

We stumbled
into it, off
a bulldozed lay-by,
its banks guarded

by the titular
April of marsh
marigold and
primrose, sorel

and wood anemone
stippling the green
sward's floodplain
of climax growth

littered by branches
of blowdown —alder,
whitethorn, oaks,
hazel, dwarf willow . . .

Up above, it seemed
straight out of
Heaney in *Sweeney
Astray*, only

the cress was missing:
ancient fragment
of birchwoods,
lichened and ungrazed,

a shoulder's touch
snapping the pristine
deadwood, all shaggy
bole in wan

shafts of sunshine,
walls and erratics
velveted with heath-moss
and violets, haggard

hosting silver birch
and gnarled trunks
of gorse, hart's tongue
betwixt stones, hollies

of hardy girth
dappling their berries
on leaf-litter as if
the folklife of dead

Diarmuid and Gráinne.
In the middle
hollow, a clearing's
mire of straw-grass

tussocks and fragrant
bayberry; by the bedrock
falls, a side-eddy
of churning turbulence

swirling foam
and gorse flowers,
sunken fern, tods
of ivy. An old

farmstead hilltop,
its whin-bushes
on the moor's edge
thick as juniper

in Arizona,
pedunculate oaks
centuries old
overhanging

stream-boulders
wedged with plastic
drink containers . . .
Later, in the dead petrol

station below the quarry,
two locals, po-faced,
knew nothing (they
owned) of any of it.

Circumpolar

At the high window nothing's changed. Irish May
Circumpolar nights the winter drew in, now gone

Into Arctic reversal. Your room's berth standing guard
As the world moves on; stilled life, the tears of things

In their carrel of memory. Outside, its darkened pane's
A single pixel on the owl's wing of our technosphere—

But inside's bright with light; and the world's distant
As a numinous Renaissance hillscape of cloud-daub

Above arrowing processionals of cypress, foregrounded
By the face of the beloved. With you, here, I remember

Aurora Borealis in Labrador—verdigris streamers
For a blackboard of String Theory—blanched Soviet nights

Along Leningrad's canals, kids in Wheatfield Avenue
My first Irish June in midsummer's jubilee of late light

Enamelling the spectrum. A world without you, all before
The time you were. At the high window *nothing's changed.*

JUNE 2004

In the Adriatic

NIGHT FERRY

Sad panda features, the old man atilt in the Full Moon:
Where is the lunar phosphorescence of the first crossing?

AUGUST GHOST

At the table on the veranda, or my laptop upstairs,
The neighbour's Amazonian green parrot haunts me

With sudden child's-cries of *Jacob!* . . . *Jacob!* . . . *Jacob!*
Mimicking, I swear, the very voice of Miriam

Trailing her brother in the garden four summers before.

KEEPSAKES

White Dalmatian sailor's cap (child-splattered), pen shell,
Partisan bullet, playing cards, Miriam's blue plastic teapot,

A piece of sea-worn copper shaped like a verdigris cedilla
Or the Mediterranean's inverted questionmark: the sacred

Objects of dead summers in the stone house at Žrnovo.

ZEPHYR

Nightmountain against the sky's lighter leaven. The Mistral
Blows through the waiting village, speaking of rainstorms

And old sorrow, bringing coolth to the limestone casement.

Near Dubrovnik

Ragusa chalked in black on the back of the chest-of-drawers
Shifted from its corner. Mid-August beer with Slobodan:

Did it first come to the house, we wonder, from Italy
During the bleak afterlife of Occupation and Resistance?

Sea-cloud

Golden-lettered, by the bowsprit of a wooden schooner,
Inevitable coinage I had never heard, or imagined:

Your memory as beautiful and distant, horizon-floating
On the blues of a thousand days launched without you.

Darwinian Scrabble

Looking down, I find the Adriatic cross-spider's back's
A crusader's tunic reminding me of the photograph

I saw once in a natural history of endangered Hawai'i
Of the *Hawaiian Happy-Face Spider* whose own amazing

Back might be whole days of life together I can't remember.

TALISMAN

This summer, a small praying mantis found its way
To the linens of Jacob's bed. It was wan and dying

But held on for three days in our makeshift glass nautilus
Before expiring clutching a bed of fennel and dead ants.

NIGHTSKY

Are they really all up there, in the Evangelical distance? True
To the thing I do—metaphor's dark matter—I see in the
    Milky Way

A badger's stripe, one ring of Saturn, its cue-ball of astrophysics.

IN THE HAMMOCK

Like death the *tremontana* came over the mountains
Out of Bosnia, empurpling the dark Balkan storm

As it did the halfmoons of your fingernails. Next day
Was rinsed-out, swept-clean clarity. Against its azure

A fractal branching of leaves in the breezy walnut
Trembled with dapple. But Angelo's almond, and the old

Hackberry at the grotto, were lost to the world forever.

LOVE

You will never return. Hope means nothing
And nothing will alter it. Love means something

Though: *you still exist for me.* Like the Big Dipper
Between the void of the two cypress, or a day moon

Against the shimmering stavelines of the heart's pylon.

THE BENCH

· We are leaving you again. The way we did
The day of the crematorium, or on the plane

To London. Your bench must weather
Another year of summer sun, winter rains,

Long nights in the maquis solitudes above
The twinking necklace of the Old Town. I feel

You're there always in the offing, waiting
An eternity for our evening walks. How lonely

The dead are, keeping time's vigil for our return.

Sea Snail

I was thinking of enchantments: Odysseus at Defora
Shouldering his ship to a strange shore, thirsty still

For life, keen for sweet water and wild boar,
Projecting the gods and forces onto the island

Of scrub-oak and Aleppo over the glistening bay.
A moment later, we find a delicate Adriatic shell,

Our most beautiful ever, back blanched and bossed,
The inner whorl the colour of a cameo's porphyry.

JULY–AUGUST 2004

[*Sic*]

I am a partisan
of the airport lounge,
disembodied

announcements
at Boarding,
revenant too

to the motorway
service station,
Stansted's cavernous

ramps, the underpass
or fly-over
past McDonald's

to the roundabout
of UK grey: those
nowhere places,

dead hibernated
spaces, in post-
modern transit

to the destinations
home job life:
arrivals and departures

in plenitudinous
spate, skating on dawn's
Bruegel-ice, chalked

quills of contrail,
Moon's
punch-hole of dayglo

gemlight. It's there
I'll meet you,
"fragile flower,"

nasturtium's fleck
fallen to the pavement,
Beslan's

theodicy
[*sic*],
on my own

journey in morning
dusk, still running
on empty.

Knin Eclogue

Out of the ten-kilometre tunnel, I was gradually
Spooked when we rose and rose into the high Lika
After its moonscape barrens: karst and mists, desolate
Woods infracted with burnt glades of spring pasture;
A thin line of gold foil threading the land's dark mirror
To dunes of a blood-orange sundown. The houses
Everywhere boarded-up but untouched, no beasts
Or ricks in the fields, no house-lights or vehicles,
Only a dimly lit neighbour in the emptied hamlet
Where the horsemen passed by. Dark Orthodox
Domes, pockmarked, inhabiting a fairy-tale desolation
Unleashed by Croatian armour; here and there
One returnee's outpost of entrepreneurial neon
New-shafting the gloom along Europa's fresh tarmac.
Someday, grief-struck, a world-after-us might look like this.

Knin Region, Croatia

In Prvo Selo

In the tradition of the place, once or more a summer,
We return to our evergreen Žrnovo door
And find hung, leant or left round the bronzed handle
Or smoothed limestone threshold, some ghost-token
Of a visitor—a bow of straw, or sheer headscarf,
Or terrace cushion, or wildflower or bough plucked
Nearby at a moment's notice. Sometimes, too, a gift
Materializes. Some tomatoes perhaps, or grappa
In a secondhand bottle, maybe a book or compote,
Lavender and oregano out of the adjacent fields,
Small cakes from a neighbour's kitchen. And if
Merely a folded piece of paper, always with neither
Name nor note. Thus out of this village silence
Immemorial as Anonymous, you come to realise
You're expected to intuit whoever it might have been
Who wished or needed seeing you at the dog day's
Missed periphery. Though once in a blue moon too,
The gift-giver or visit, like a ghost guested all summer,
Asked after, stays unknown despite the guesswork.

"The Sarajevo Music-box"

Where did it come from? Sarajevo, maybe? So
We stuck with that and named it thus, a memory
Reappearing, out of the blue, one year on—and from
Thenceforwards my lamp-side icon, or sad *madeleine*,
For all that's lost or forgotten, or once was missed.
There's something homespun and provisional about it,
Non-commodified and Communist, something old-world
In some way suggesting Tito's bygone *Mitteleuropa*
In varnished woodform. At any rate, you loved it:
The little tune and car-crank handle-knob,
The four stovepiped heads and plastic porthole
Revealing its wooden innards. You wound it round
Endlessly at Sally's. And behind it, often enough,
There hangs the reminiscence of a Berlin moment,
December '89, gone East across from Kreuzberg
With two new-found friends, when Matthias took us
For a dusky hour along a muted street of Eastern tenements
Ending in the Wall, threadbare but somehow rich
In age and atmosphere; whereupon we entered
His after-hours, one-room kindergarten sanctum
For art activities. No rent of course, and well
Below the radar; but a bracing hard-earned spirit-scent
Therein, like the wintry breath we'd carried in
Out of the chill evening, threshold-lit; possessed of nothing
But parents' love, *papier-mâché* puppets, evergreen boughs,
Plain white walls. And beyond it all, banished by the real
Wall of Separation, gone over into nothing, unnameable in all
But name, the life that gave it life has vanished just the same.

After Hay-on-Wye

I remember leaving Wales
through lush English
Herefordshire, heart-sore
and soul-sick—the road before

and the same behind, straddled
with light and shadow,
the hay-scents and hot May day
falling wordlessly away

in the wake of your receding
time, receding still—face-forward
after Hay-on-Wye—through the heart's
rear window or rushing carriage-heat.

MARCH 2006

Coda

They are still around us, the dead, but there are times when I think that perhaps they will soon be gone. Now that we have reached the point where the number of those alive on earth has doubled within just three decades, and will treble within the next generation, we need no longer fear the once overwhelming numbers of the dead. Their significance is visibly decreasing. We can no longer speak of everlasting memory and the veneration of forebears. On the contrary: the dead must now be cleared out of the way as quickly and comprehensively as possible. What mourner at a crematorium funeral has not thought, as the coffin moves into the furnace, that the way we now take leave of the dead is marked by ill-concealed and paltry haste? And the room allotted to them becomes smaller and smaller; they are often given notice to leave after only a few years. Where will their mortal remains go then, how will they be disposed of? It is a fact that there is great pressure on space, even here in the country. What must it be like in the cities inexorably moving towards the thirty million mark? Where will they all go, the dead of Buenos Aires and Sao Paulo, of Mexico City, Lagos and Cairo, Toyko, Shanghai and Bombay? Very few of them, probably, into a cool grave. And who has remembered them, who remembers them at all? To remember, to retain and to preserve, Pierre Bertraux wrote of the mutation of mankind even thirty years ago, was vitally important only when population density was low, we manufactured few items, and nothing but space was present in abundance. You could not do without anyone then, even after death. In the urban societies of the late twentieth century, on the other hand, where everyone is instantly replaceable and is really superfluous from birth, we have to keep throwing ballast overboard, forgetting everything that we might otherwise remember: youth, childhood, our origins, our forebears and ancestors. For a while the site called the Memorial Grove recently set up on the Internet may endure; here you can lay those particularly close to you to rest electronically and visit them. But this virtual cemetery too will dissolve into the ether, and the whole past will flow into a formless, indistinct, silent mass. And leaving a present without memory, in the face of a future that no individual mind can now envisage, in the end we shall ourselves relinquish life without feeling any need to linger at least for a while, nor shall we be impelled to pay return visits from time to time.

W. G. SEBALD, *Campo Santo*